The Revival You Want.
The Revival You Need!

...the astonish account of the Hebrides Revival
and the strategies we can implement

Rick Leland
Duncan Campbell

Copyright © 2023 Rick Leland

All rights reserved.

ISBN: 979-8-9890957-1-1

Published By:
Red River Media
Nada, Kentucky
rick@rickleland.com
rickleland.com

All rights reserved. No part of this book may be reproduced or transmitted in any form or means. Electronic or mechanical. With out written permission.

Scripture References are from the Holy Bible as follows:

King James Version

The New King James Version, Copywrite 1984 by Thomas Nelson. Used by permission.

Sermon from Duncan Campbell: public domain work used for research.

DEDICATION

"You can tell a lot about a man
by the way he builds his fire."

In Gratitude:
Chelsea Nolan
Pastor Lindell Cooley
Pastor Alvena Smith

CONTENTS

	Introduction	Pg. 1
1.	Recipe for Revival	Pg. 5
2.	Crying Out to God	Pg. 21
3.	The Breakthrough	Pg. 27
4.	The Spreading of the Miracle Move of God	Pg. 39
5.	Characteristics of Revival	Pg. 47
6.	Opposition Arises. Opposition Falls	Pg. 59
7.	Changing a Community	Pg. 71
8.	A True Story. A True Revival	Pg. 87
	Epilogue. A Beginning, Not an End	Pg. 89
	Adios	Pg. 97

Introduction

In the Christian church world, the word *revival* would have a wide spectrum of meanings.

Recently, I was involved in revival meetings on the westside of Louisville, Kentucky with True Believers in Christ Church. And then three days later I had the honor of meeting Lindell Cooley, who was the worship/song leader of the Brownsville Revival.

Both are called revivals. I heard Pastor Alvena say, kind of as a target, that she was hoping for one person during the five days of meetings to get saved. Now her church is small and essentially the budget was zero.

Now at Brownsville, thousands and thousands of people became followers of Jesus Christ. Brownsville went six years and was, in every fashion, radically different from the True Believer's revival services.

One thing I know is that God moved and touched people in both places.

I would also say undoubtedly, each church utilized

some of the same tools God has given us to further His kingdom, make Him known, and glorify His Great Name, the Name of Jesus, and to inflame the power of the Holy Spirit.

In *The Revival You Want. The Revival You Need!* I am going to examine the Hebrides Revival, helping us to glean some lessons on revival. My focus is going to be on what I am calling the *unplanned revival*, rather than the scheduled type revival. Yet, there will be plenty of crossover application to use for this type of meeting. Because God uses the scheduled type and can, let's say, "Blow the doors off of your plans."

The Hebrides Revival is less known than an entire list of more name-brandish revivals over the years. It is likely you have never heard of it.

The Hebrides Revival took place from 1949 through 1953 on the Hebrides Island off the north-west coast of Scottland. A key player in the revival was Duncan Campbell, who was a college student, yet already had a known preaching ministry.

The story part of the book comes from a sermon Campbell preached in September 1968. And then I will add application, insight, and commentary to make this book's aim to be a resource for enhancing the effectiveness of any style of revival. Regarding Campbell's telling of the story, I will sparingly, smooth out some of his words to add clarity. And then, as far as my author's notes are concerned, it will be necessary to change names and a few details for privacy and other reasons. Neither author-tool will change the truth even in the slightest.

I realize that there is a certain contingent who has already checked out because I have mentioned the Brownsville Revival. Do not do it. That is all I need to say. The blood is on you.

One more thing before we dive into the awe-inspiring accounts of the Hebrides Revival, we need to acknowledge that some people set the bar extremely high in terms of what they did to usher in, advance, and maintain this spectacular move of God.

If you were a pole vaulter and your best effort was five feet, it would not be wise to raise the bar to the world record heighth of 20'2" set by Mondo Duplantis. Why beat yourself up and charge forward towards certain failure? God is merciful. He loves you and will accept you at the level you are at.

If You seek Him and press in, he will empower you to go higher. And like Mondo Duplantis, when he set the world record, always pause, and give God some glory for any uptick.

This is something I truly love about God. His mercy in conjunction with the place we are in our lives, yet His mercy also wants us to grow.

My prayer is that *The Revival You Want. The Revival You Need!* will help you reach one more, one more, one more, one more…for the kingdom of God.

Psalm 85:5-6
"Will You not revive us again, that Your people may rejoice in You? Show us Your mercy, LORD and grant us Your salvation."

Chapter 1.

Recipe for Revival

There are two things that I, Duncan Campbell would like to say in speaking about the revival in the Hebrides. First, I would like to make it perfectly clear that I did not bring revival to the Hebrides.

It has grieved me beyond words to hear people talk and write about the man who brought revival to the Hebrides. My dear people, I did not do that. Revival was there before I ever set foot on the island. It began in a gracious awareness of God sweeping through the parish of Barvas on the Hebrides Island.

Also, I would like to make it perfectly clear of what I understand regarding the concept of revival. When I speak of revival, I am not thinking of high-pressure evangelism. I am not referring to crusades or of special efforts convened and organized by man. That is not in my mind at all.

Revival is something altogether different from evangelism on its highest level. Revival is a moving of God in the community and suddenly the community becomes God-conscious. Even before a word is said by any man representing any special effort.

Now, I am sure that you will be interested to know how, in November 1949, this gracious movement began on the island of Lewis.

Two old women, one of them 84 years of age and the other 82 and one of them stone-blind, were greatly burdened because of the appalling state of their own parish. It was true that not a single young person attended public worship. Not a single young man or young woman went to the church. They spent their day perhaps reading or walking, but the church was left out of the picture.

And those two women were greatly concerned, and they made it a special matter of prayer.

A Bible verse gripped them: "I will pour water on him that is thirsty and floods upon the dry ground," from Isaiah 44:3.

They were so burdened that both of them decided to spend much time in prayer twice a week. On

Tuesday, they got on their knees at 10 o'clock in the evening and remained on their knees until 3 or 4 o'clock in the morning—two old women in a very humble cottage.

One night, one of the sisters had a vision. Now remember, in revival, God works in wonderful ways. A vision came to one of them. In the vision, she saw the church of her father crowded with young people. Packed to the doors with a strange minister standing in the pulpit.

She was so impressed by the vision that she sent for the parish minister. Familiar with the two sisters' deep connection with God, he gladly accepted their invitation and traveled to the cottage.

That morning, one of the sisters said to the minister, "You must do something about it. I would suggest that you call your elders together and that you spend with us at least two nights in prayer this week. Tuesday and Friday, if you gather your elders and deacons together, you can meet in a barn in the farming community. You can meet in a barn and as you pray there, we will pray here."

Well, that was what happened. The minister called

for his elders and deacons. Seven of them met in a barn to pray on Tuesday and on Friday. And the two old women got on their knees and prayed with them.

Well, that continued for some weeks—indeed, I believe almost a month and a half. Until one night; now this is what I am eager for you to get a hold of. One night they were kneeling there in the barn, pleading this promise, "I will pour water on him that is thirsty, floods upon the dry ground."

When one young man, a deacon in the church, got up and read Psalm 24, "Who shall ascend the hill of God? Who shall stand in His holy place? He that has clean hands and a pure heart who has not lifted up his soul unto vanity or sworn deceitfully. He shall receive the blessing (not a blessing, but the blessing) of the Lord."

Then that young man closed his Bible and looking down at the minister and the other office bearers.

He said this; maybe crude words, but perhaps not so crude in our Gaelic language; he said, "It seems to me to be so much humbug to be praying as we are praying, to be waiting as we are waiting, if we ourselves are not rightly related to God."

And then he lifted his two hands, and I'm telling you, just as the minister told me it happened, he lifted his two hands and prayed, "God, are my hands clean? Is my heart pure?"

But he got no further. That young man fell to his knees and then fell into a trance. Now do not ask me to explain this because I cannot.

He fell into a trance and was lying on the floor of the barn. And the minister, at that moment, he and his deacons and elders were gripped by the conviction that a God-sent revival must always be related to holiness, must always be related to Godliness. Are my hands clean? Is my heart pure? The man that God will trust with revival must be holy, must be Godly. Now that was the conviction.

When that happened in the barn, the power of God swept into the parish. And an awareness of God gripped the community such as had not been known for over one hundred years. An awareness of God—that's revival, that's revival! And on the following day, the looms were silent. They did little work on the farms as men and women gave themselves to pondering on eternal things and gripped with eternal realities.

Author's Note One:

It would be easy to be awestruck by the Hebrides Revival. It is like enjoying the warmth but freezing up when it comes to receiving any impartation for raising the bar in our lives.

How about one more inch, one more person?

One more inch—resolve to, by the mercy of God, to march unwaveringly up the mountain of God, to a higher plain of seeking, advancing, maintaining true God-driven revival.

One more inch.

One more person—the heartbeat of God. The searching for the one in our peripheral who needs the revival touch.

And then taking the step of faith to be God's loving servant to reach out.

One more person.

Chapter one includes most of the recipe for revival.

Maybe the whole recipe and a few sprinkles for extra zest.

1. Humility.

Duncan Campell does not even launch off without setting the record straight and humbling himself. He could have easily left that part off, but we see as he continues with his account that humility is woven into the entire story. No genuine humility; no real revival—bottom line.

2. God uses the unlikely.

So, we have two old women who were sisters. One is eighty-two, and the other is eighty-four. And one of them is blind. Campbell does not even recognize them by name. These are the two that lit the flame.

The precious words from the second half of 2 Samuel 16:7 is defined by these Holy Spirit empowered ladies, "For the LORD does not see as man sees; for man looks at the outward appearance, but the LORD looks at the heart."

We are not very good at this. At least that is my observation.

There is a church I have attended probably a dozen times. Good church; the pastor is well-known—I appreciate his preaching.

Yet he has this strange thing he does. He gravitates to other famous people and then makes it known from the pulpit. And then down the road, he figures out they are heretics and then he recants his relationship, again from the pulpit.

Yet I have repeatedly heard him telling of *nobodies* coming to him saying they were on assignment from God or offered something in writing. He then asserts his effective discernment, so he brushes off the nobodies as screwballs. And likely most fall into that category.

I have heard him repeatedly mentioning this scenario, but never once, heard him pump it up for a total odd-ball who was genuinely sent from God.

Not one sent from God?

That is impossible. Guaranteed.

Are you a person with some sway, maybe a lot of sway in the church world and you slather over the famous, yet the eighty-four-year-old lady and her blind sister, with no presence on Facebook, you instantly dismiss as yawners?

Not good. Not God. God uses the unlikely.

3. Get a promise from God.

Throughout the retelling of the story of the Hebrides Revival, the first part of the verse from Isaiah 44:3, "For I will pour water on him who is thirsty, and floods on the dry ground," is cited as a promise from God.

The sisters grabbed a hold of this promise ferociously.

It says that this passage gripped the two fire starters.

I read the Bible every day. I have for twenty-five plus years, so I have read this verse at least twenty-times. Yet, I never once thought to myself that this half a Bible verse could unleash massive waves of God's life changing power over my community.

Still, it became a promise from God. Which we will see later, they hammered the throne of God with.

That is a head shaker. And I feel inadequate to verbalize how this could happen, and Campbell does not offer any additional insight.

This one thing I am sure of, this supernatural promise from God did not grip the heroes of the revival via casual pursuit, even significant pursuit, but only by radical, intense pursuit of the heart of God. With much sacrifice and crying out to God. Something this precious takes a lot of toil.

I have this mental picture of the eighty-plus year-old lady, with a pole in her hand. She is staring at the bar set at 20'3".

"He who dwells in the secret place of the Most High Shall abide under the shadow of the Almighty."

A promise that bold can only be revealed in the Secret Place.

4. Prayer.

Have you ever been on your knees in prayer for five hours? Five hours!

Undoubtedly, the prayer was the foundation on which they built the Hebrides Revival. And the ones who laid the foundation were these two elderly women of God.

There is no hint in Campbell's telling of the story of what transpired in those five-hour blocks of prayer. But for starters, a prayer session like this is where they detected the promise they stood on as they went boldly before the throne of God, with grisly tenacity.

Is it possible to preach enough sermons and endure enough Bible studies to get to this level of prayer?

I am going to say, "No."

The fuel for five hours of crying out to God, tear filled travailing prayers, and acutely focused intercessory prayer for individuals would have transpired from a love for God and a love for people. Mixed with a staunch faith that they would receive answered prayers.

The last part of Matthew 24:12 says, "The love of many will grow cold."

For those of us who want to pursue revival, our refrain needs to be, "The love of us few will grow hotter—for God, for people.

5. The Supernatural

Cambell tells of one of the elderly ladies having a vision and later of a young man falling into a trance and in a subsequent chapter, more visions will be mentioned. We can only see these as supernatural. Something given by God. And they play an important function in stirring and maintaining the revival.

Cambell notes in upcoming chapters that they did not see some of the miracles/supernatural which often accompany revivals—such as healings and the flow of gifts of the Holy Spirit.

It would be unlikely to find a significant revival without supernatural miracles. So, if God wants to incorporate these in revivals, we need to tap into these God-implemented means to reach more people.

6. Unity. Being in One Accord.

The power of being in one accord/unity does not get much air time in the church presently. Plenty of chatter about the opposite.

The best example is the hundred and twenty in the upper room. The Bible says they were in one accord. It was important enough for God to note it as a characteristic of the power-move that exploded from the place of one accord, then going forth to change the world.

I do not think we fully grasp how powerful being in one accord is regarding launching a revival into existence.

I was at a small man-planned type revival (God can use these) that was to run five days. From day one to day two, you could sense momentum building. And then a group of people came in on the third night. They mocked one of the musicians when his quality was not up to their standard and were very frivolous in their actions. To the degree of being flippant.

So that night, which was night three, there was a distinctive downturn.

The next night, only one person from the group returned. I was upfront early on during the next evening, and as tactfully as possible; I put my spiritual foot down to stop the disunity.

That night was the best night of the revival by far, up to that point, and the next night was the highlight of the meetings.

In Campbell's retelling, the sister's request caused the number of people praying and trusting in God's promise to grow from two to nine.

Nine people were on their knees, focused on what God had spoken into their hearts. They were in one accord. And we can see what happened.

My thinking is, if just two people are in one accord, start there and build.

7. Holiness

What a beautiful picture of revelation the young deacon received; realizing without holiness, they were praying in vain. From there, conviction and repentance completed the trifecta. A combination that is essential for unlocking revival.

There are many stories about how just one person's conviction and repentance roused a revival-type move of God.

The Bible says in more than one place, "Be holy, because I am (God) holy."

Not an option when you are seeking true God-fueled revival.

I know at Brownsville; they were fastidious regarding holiness—from the top down.

Holiness is power for those who embrace it and legalism for those who do not truly understand God's heart in the matter.

Personally, I pursue holiness because I love God and I love people.

If God needs to chasten us, to enable the pouring out of the full-measure of His power, I will get in that line any day.

There is room for you.

Psalm 24:3-5

"Who may ascend into the hill of the LORD? Or who may stand in His holy place? He who has clean hands and a pure heart, who has not lifted up his

soul to an idol, nor sworn deceitfully. He shall receive a blessing from the LORD, Your salvation."

Chapter2.

Crying Out to God

Now, I was not on the island when things first started happening.

But one sister sent for the minister and she said to him, "I think you ought to invite someone to the parish. I cannot give a name, but God must have someone in His mind, for we saw a strange man in the pulpit and that man must be somewhere."

Well, the minister that week was going to one of our great conventions in Scotland. At that convention he met a young man who was a student in college and knowing that this young man was a God-fearing man, a man with a message, he invited him to the island.

"Won't you come for ten days—a ten-day special effort? We have had so many of them over the past couple of years, but we feel that something is happening in the parish and we would like you to attend."

This minister said, "No, I don't feel that I am the man, but recently there has been a very remarkable move in Glasgow under the ministry of a man by the name of Duncan Campbell. I would suggest that you send for him."

Now at that time I was in a college in Edinburgh. It was not very easy for me to leave, but I decided I should go for ten days. So, I arrived on the island within ten days.

I shall never forget the night that I arrived at the piers in the mail steamer. I was standing in the minister's presence whom I had never seen and two of his elders that I did not know.

The minister turned to me and said, "I know, Mr. Campbell, that you are exhausted; you have been traveling all day by train to begin with and then by steamer. And I am sure that you are ready for your supper and ready for your bed. But I wonder if you would be prepared to address a meeting in the parish church at 9 o'clock tonight on our way home. It will be a short meeting and then we will go to the parsonage. Then you will get your supper and your bed and you can rest until tomorrow evening."

Well, it will interest you to know that I never got supper that night.

We got to the church about a quarter to nine to find about three hundred people gathered. I would say about three hundred people and I gave an address.

Nothing really happened during the service. It was a good meeting. A sense of God, a consciousness of His Spirit moving, but nothing beyond that. So, I pronounced the benediction, and we were leaving the church about a quarter to eleven.

Just as I am walking down the aisle, along with this young deacon who read the Psalm in the barn.

Suddenly he stood in the aisle and looking up to the heavens, he said, "God, You can't fail us. God, You can't fail us! You promised to pour water on the thirsty and floods upon the dry ground-God, You can't fail us!"

Soon he is on his knees in the aisle. He is still praying and then he falls into a trance again.

Author's Note Two:

We can glean a couple of revival enhancing strategies from this chapter.

1. Bring in re-enforcements. Bring in the right person.

The revival was breaking out. Instead of relying solely on the island's ministers, they recognized the need for someone else to step in and advance the move of God.

Of course, these praying sisters were so in tune with God that He gave them a vision to highlight this key strategy.

Still, many people would be resistant and would want to guard their position in this move of God. Thanks be to God, these were humble people who had pure motivations.

Jostling for position rather than seeking the heart of God will snuff out a genuine move of God overnight. I have heard the stories.

2. Crying out to God

We find the concept of crying out to God throughout the Bible. In distress, need, and want; cry out to God.

And not only is the young deacon crying out to God, but it would be hard not to see that his words went beyond crying out and he was effectively calling God out. Putting a demand on God.

Hebrews 4:16 "Let us therefore come boldly to the throne of grace, that we may obtain mercy and find grace to help in time of need."

It says to come boldly, yet not exactly giving the sense of being bombastic.

Still, we see in Exodus 14 Moses gets audacious with God, and for all intent, tells God if He doesn't change His mind, He's going to look bad. Very demanding.

This is my sense and experience, if you are in the secret place with God, living a holy life, valiantly pursuing God's purpose for your life; this type of relationship allows a person to know how and when to press God into moving forth.

I am less than a journeyman in exploring this relational concept, yet I have experienced one important healing miracle in part because I would not relent. I am big on the proper fear of the LORD (not just awe), yet there is a way to press God with humility and vigor simultaneously.

It will be crucial for those seeking historic levels of revival to aim higher in this area.

Numbers 14:17
"And now, I pray, let the power of my Lord be great..."

Chapter 3.

The Breakthrough

Just then, the door opened—it was now eleven o'clock.

The door of the church opens and the local blacksmith comes back into the church and says, "Mr. Campbell, something wonderful has happened. Oh, we prayed God would pour water on the thirsty and floods upon the dry ground and listen, He's done it! He's done it!"

When I went to the door of the church. I saw a congregation of approximately six hundred people. Six hundred people—where had they come from? What had happened? I believe that very night God swept in Pentecostal power, the power of the Holy Ghost. And what had happened in the early days of the apostles was now happening in the parish of Barvas.

Over one hundred young people were at the dance in the parish hall, and they were not thinking of

God or eternity. God was not at all in their thoughts. They were there to have a good night, when suddenly the power of God fell upon the dance. The music ceased and in a matter of minutes; the hall was empty. They fled from the hall as a man fleeing from a plague and they made their way to the church. They are now standing outside.

Oh yes, they saw lights in the church. A house of God and they were going to it and they went. Men and women who had gone to bed rose, dressed, and made for the church. Nothing in the way of publicity; no mention of a special event, except a mention from the pulpit on Sunday that a certain man was going to be conducting a series of meetings in the parish, covering ten days.

But God took the situation in hand. Oh, He became His own publicity agent. A hunger and a thirst gripped the people. Six hundred of them are now at the church—standing outside.

This dear man, the blacksmith, turned to me and said, "I think we should sing a psalm."

So they sang, and they sang, and they sang verse after verse. Oh, what singing! What singing! And then they opened the doors, and the congregation rushed back into the church.

Now, people have crowded the church. A church that seats over eight hundred is now packed to capacity.

It is now nearing midnight. I managed to make my way through the crowd along the aisle toward the pulpit.

I found a young woman, a teacher in the grammar school, lying prostrate on the floor of the pulpit praying, "Oh, God, is there mercy for me? Oh, God, is there mercy for me? "

She was one of those at the dance. But she is now lying on the floor of the pulpit, crying to God for mercy.

That meeting continued until 4 o'clock in the morning. I could not tell you how many were saved that night, but of this I am sure and certain that at least five young men who were saved in that church that night, are today ministers in the church of Scotland, having gone through the university and college.

At 4 o'clock, we made our way to the parsonage. Of course, you understand, we made no appeals. You never need to make an appeal or an altar call in revival.

Why, the roadside becomes an altar. We just leave men and women to make their way to God themselves—after all, that is the right way. God can look after His own. Oh, God can look after His own! And when God takes a situation in hand, I tell you He does a better work. He does a better job.

So we left them there and just as I was leaving the church, a young man came to me.

And he said, "Mr. Campbell, I would like you to go to the police station."

I said, "The police station? What's wrong?"

"Oh," he said, "There's nothing wrong, but there must be at least four hundred people gathered around the police station just now."

Now the sergeant there was a God-fearing man. He was in the meeting and people knew that this was a house that feared God. And next to the police station was the cottage in which the two old women lived. I believe that had something to do with the magnet, the power that drew men.

There was a coach load at that meeting. A coach load had traveled over twelve miles to be there. Now, if anyone would ask them today, why? How did it happen? Who arranged it? They could not tell you.

But they found themselves grouping together and someone said, "What about going to Barvas? I don't know, but I have a hunger in my heart to go there."

I cannot explain it. They could not explain it. But God had the situation in hand.

This is revival dear people! This is a sovereign act of God! This is the moving of God's Spirit. I believe it was an answer to the prevailing prayers of men and women who believed that God was a covenant-keeping God who must be true to His covenant agreement.

I went along. I went along to that meeting. As I was walking along that country road, we had to walk about a mile. I heard someone praying by the roadside. I could hear this man crying to God for mercy. I went over and there were four young men on their knees on the roadside. Yes, they were at the dance, but they are now crying to God for mercy.

One of them was under the influence of drink. A young man who was less than twenty years of age. But that night God saved him and today he is the parish minister—university trained, college trained man of God. Converted in the revival along with eleven of his elders and deacons. A wonderful congregation. That night, he received salvation.

Now when I got to the police station, I saw something that will live with me as long as I live. I did not preach. There was no need for preaching. We did not even sing. The people are crying to God for mercy. Oh, the confessions that were made!

There was one old man crying out, "Oh, God, hell is too good for me! Hell is too good for me!"

This is Holy Ghost conviction! Now, mind you, that was on the very first night of a mighty demonstration that shook the island.

Oh, let me say again, that was not the beginning of revival. Revival began in a prayer, bartering meeting. Revival began with an awareness of God.

Revival began when the Holy Ghost began to grip men.

And that was how it began.

Author's Note Three:

The events unfolding in the Hebrides Revival are so astonishing that they seem unreal, and if real, impossible to achieve.

They are undeniably real and certainly these pinnacle-achieving examples could make us seem like a fifth grader trying to win the Olympic Marathon.

But remember, we do not have to run or win their race. Our focus needs to be: one more inch, one more person.

And like Philippians 3:14 says, "I press toward the goal for the prize of the upward call of God in Christ Jesus." Always upward is our focus.

So here are some ascending fueled takeaways from this chapter.

1. Time

Time constraints are a weapon opposing true revival. This does not mean God cannot use a revival with days and times planned out. This scenario is like the fire in a metal ringed fire pit, which is a controlled burn. But it is still burning and certainly better than no fire at all. Way better.

Now the no time constraint format is more like letting the Holy Spirit blow the flames of revival to whatever degree and direction God sees fit. Could get a little wild.

Think of the Hebrides Revival. Night one for the visiting preacher, Duncan Campbell, the meeting goes from 8:45 p.m. to 4:00 a.m. And according to his own words, he did not have supper that evening.

The sacrifice is considerable; likely, one of the defining dynamics as far as the impact/success of a revival.

2. Worship through singing and music.

I would love to have heard the singing Campbell refers to as, "Oh, what singing! What singing!"

Imagine the vibrance of this singing as their passion for Jesus was spiraling; as it set ablaze revival fires. The power of worship music is well known, still it always amazes me why more people don't sing to our LORD with more gusto. It is not solely about the energy level, but how much of our heart yearns to exalt our triune God. Music is an unparalleled form of expression in worship.

David in the Bible basically danced before God, in a pair of modest swimming trunks; dancing, with extravagant expression. It was not a show; it was his heart.

I cannot fathom how people can sit passively in the midst of an occasion to worship God. No serious revival will be devoid of passionate, upward focused worship via music. Being undignified and caring only what God thinks, is a weighty force for advancing revival.

3. Let God do the work.

Duncan Campbell said it well, "When God takes a situation in hand, I tell you, He does a better work."

I can think of three revivals I know of, Holy Spirit infused ones, in which man put his hand on what God was doing, and they died quickly. Not to agree with what they did, still it is a monumental challenge to know the balance point—sensing how to manage, without quenching the Holy Spirit.

While usually it is the top-church leaders who decide, yet someone fine-tuned into the things of God, like the elderly sisters, could offer better guidance. Oh, for more humility to listen to those types of God-lovers.

4. Mercy.

Mercy comes from God. And conviction of the Holy Spirit is paramount for instigating the crying out for mercy. True crying out for mercy, unquestionably, is a sweet sound in God's ear.

Having people in a revival, desperately seeking the mercy of God, seems to be the byproduct of carrying out other components of the revival well. Of course, one person seeking God's mercy can stir a whole multitude.

And then, in the throes of revival, great mercy needs to come forth for those attending, from those who are shepherding the move of God.

Psalm 143:11
"Revive me, O LORD, for Your name's sake! For Your righteousness' sake, bring my soul out of trouble!"

Chapter 4.

The Spreading of the Miracle Move of God

And, of course, after that we were at it night and day, and the churches were crowded.

I remember one night it was after 3 o'clock in the morning; a messenger came to say that the churches were crowded in another parish of Lewis, which was fifteen miles away. Crowded at that hour in the morning.

So I went to that parish minister, along with several other ministers. I thank God for the ministers of Lewis, for how they responded to the call of God. How they threw themselves into the effort. And God blessed them for it.

We went, and I preached in a large church. A church that seated a thousand and the Spirit of God was moving—oh, moving in a mighty way! I could see them falling, falling on their knees. I could hear them crying to God for mercy. I could hear those outside praying.

This continued for, I am sure, two hours.

Then, as we were leaving the church, someone came to me to tell me that a very large number of people had gathered on a field because they could not get into the church. They could not get into any of the churches. So, they had gathered in a field.

Along with the other ministers, I decided to go to the field and there I saw an enormous crowd standing there as though gripped by a power that they could not explain.

But the interesting thing about that meeting was a sight that I saw. The headmaster of a secondary school in the parish is lying on his face on the ground crying to God for mercy. Oh, deeply convicted of his desperate need and on either side of him were two young girls. I would say about sixteen years of age—two on each side of him.

And they kept saying to the headmaster, "Master Jesus that saved us last night in Barvas, can save you in Lewis tonight. Jesus that saved us last night in Barvas can save you tonight."

It is true that when a person comes into vital relationship with Jesus Christ, their supreme desire is to win others. To win others! And they were there that night to win their master and they won him. Oh, God swept into his life. I believe in answer to the prayer of four young girls, sixteen years of age, who had a burden. Who had a burden!

Now that was how the revival began, and that is how it continued for five weeks. The first wave of the revival continued for five weeks, and then there was a lull. Perhaps a lull of about a week.

The churches remain crowded, as people continue to seek after God and were holding prayer meetings all over the parishes.

It was the custom in those parishes that those who found the Savior at night would be at a prayer meeting at noonday. A prayer meeting met every day and noonday. At that time all work stopped for two hours—looms were silent. For two hours, work stopped in the fields and men gathered for prayer. And it was then that you got to know those who had found the Savior on the previous night.

You did not need to make an appeal. They made their way to the prayer meeting to praise God for His salvation.

This continued for almost three years. Until the whole of the island was swept by the mighty power of God. I could not tell you how many. I never checked the numbers. I was afraid to do that, always remembering what David did. I left the records with God. But this I know, that at least seventy-five percent of those who were born again during the revival were born again before they came near a church. Before they had any word from me or any of the other ministers.

I can think just now of a certain village, the village of Weaver, and there was a row of cottages by the roadside. There were seven of them altogether and in every cottage a loom and a weaver. One morning, just as the men were being called for breakfast, they discovered that the seven of them were lying prostrate behind their looms. Lying on their faces behind their looms and all of them in a trance. Now I cannot explain this. But of this I am certain, this was of God because the seven men were saved that day. Now, I should say six of them were saved that day, one of them on the following day.

But they came to understand that something supernatural from God had taken possession of them. An awareness of God gripped them and a hunger seized them and they cried out to God for mercy. And God swept in.

I was visiting those weavers recently. I was up in the Hebrides and what a joy it was to listen to them retell of that wonderful experience. The experience of when God swept into those seven houses.

My dear people, that's revival! I mean, it is so different from our special efforts, our planned meetings. So dissimilar altogether from man's best endeavor.

God is in the middle, and miracles happen!

Author's Note 4:

Let me highlight two lasting impressions from this chapter.

1. Hunger and perseverance.

Hunger and perseverance are twin mast heads for keeping a revival sailing along. Hunger and perseverance intertwine inseparably.

It's 3 a.m. The churches are packed with people. So, you find a hill and an *enormous* crowd gathers to cry out for God. Are you slightly dumbfounded at this point, like I am?

Did the bar just go from 20'2"to 25'?

OK, let's get un-dumbfounded.

One more inch.

One more person.

I am not ready for the 25' vault, but dear Lord empower me, by your Holy Spirit, to reach higher and wider as I seek to increase my hunger and perseverance for the things of God. Oh God, I need you! More than yesterday!

2. Heart for the lost—a heart to win souls

All revivals, of any type or size, need to revolve around the central theme of expanding the kingdom of God through evangelism to those who don't know Jesus.

While it is amazing that in the Hebrides Revival, Campbell asserts no appeals were required for those who did not know Jesus. This is extremely rare. Extremely rare.

So, does it really need to be said? Preach the Gospel of Jesus Christ! Make the appeal to the lost.

> Proverbs 11:30b
> "He who wins souls is wise."

Chapter 5.

Characteristics of Revival

Now perhaps I should go into some features that characterized this remarkable movement.

Already I have mentioned to you that we found men in trances. Perhaps I should say this: in the Hebrides revival, we never saw anybody healed. That was not a feature of it. We never heard anybody speaking in tongues—in a strange language. Personally, I heard nobody speak in tongues until a year or two ago. And that was in England. We knew nothing about such manifestations.

Don't misunderstand me, I believe in every gift mentioned in the word of God. But it wasn't God's plan or purpose that we should be visited in that way and we weren't.

Still, we saw strange manifestations.

I think just now of a certain island that up until then God hadn't moved on this island. One of the smaller islands, perhaps an island of six-hundred souls. And they asked me to go to this island to officiate at a communion. Now, a communion in Lewis is just like one of your conventions. They begin with a prayer meeting on Wednesday night. Then on Thursday, schools are closed, shops are closed, no work is done. It is just like another Sunday. That is Thursday.

Friday is then testimony day when men give their testimonies. They ask the women to be silent. You will never hear a woman give her testimony at such meetings. But the men speak; however, I am glad to say that many of the dear women got glorious liberty during the revival. And they are meeting for prayer and are praying with the men today. That is a transformation that has taken place subsequent to the revival.

So I am on this smaller island and I felt the going fearfully hard. Oh, it was difficult to preach. You felt your very words coming back and hitting you. And I was a bit distressed.

I turned to one of the other ministers and I said, "Now don't you think we should send for the praying men of Barvas?"

Let me say in passing that the praying men of Barvas were praying for us just then. There were at least five of them in this part of God's vineyard who promised to do that, and I believe they were keeping to their promise.

However, I sent for them and in a conversation I had with this businessman, who was one of the praying men, I said, "If it is at all possible, will you bring little Donald McInnes."

Now I will tell you later how Donald came to know the Lord. So I asked them to bring Donald McInnes to the island.

Now Donald had a remarkable experience on the hillside two weeks after he was born again. And God came upon him. The Holy Ghost came upon him. He had a mighty baptism.

I hope you believe in the baptism of the Holy Ghost as a distinct experience. You may disagree, but I believe in it. I do not think that I am preaching one set of doctrines that insists upon gifts.

I am not thinking of that at all, because I believe that the baptism of the Holy Ghost, in its final analysis, is just the revelation of Jesus. It is Jesus becoming real—wonderful, powerful, and dynamic in a person's life. And He then expresses Himself through our personality. That is the baptism of the Holy Ghost that I believe in.

Not that I disbelieve in other experiences. Of course, I don't. Some of my dearest friends are among those who exercise the gifts.

But that said, this young fellow had such a baptism of God among the heather bushes that he forgot about coming home. So, a search party had to be sent out to find him in the hills.

And they found him on his face among the bushes repeating over and over, "Oh, Jesus, I love You. Oh, Jesus I love You."

And wasn't he near to Jesus if he spoke like that? Of course he was.

Well, I asked the men to bring little Donald with them. Then we are in the service at the church.

And I am preaching from the text from Isaiah 63:1, "Who is this that cometh from Edom, with dyed garments from Bozrah? This that is glorious in his apparel, travelling in the greatness of his strength? I that speak in righteousness, mighty to save."

But oh, I tell you, the going was hard. The going was hard.

I looked down, and I saw little Donald sitting there in the seat. I saw little Donald sitting there in the seat, with his head bowed and tears wetting the floor.

And I said to myself, "Well, now, there is a young lad nearer to God than you or I. Oh, there is a young lad who is in touch with God."

And I stopped preaching. Looking down at this young lad, I said, "Donald, I believe God would have you lead us in prayer."

It was right in the midst of my address. So that young lad stood to his feet.

Now that morning at family worship they were reading Revelation 4, where John has the vision of the open door. "I saw a door opened in heaven."

And as Donald stood, that vision came before him and this is what he said in his prayers, "God, I seem to be gazing in through the open door and I seem to see the Lamb standing in the midst of the throne. He has the keys of death and of hell in his hand."

Then he stopped and began to weep. And for a minute or so, he wept, and he wept. Oh, the brokenness. And when he was able to control himself.

He lifted his eyes towards the heavens and he cried out, "God, there is power there! Let it loose! Let it loose!"

Suddenly, the power of God fell upon the congregation.

Of course, in Lewis and in other islands of the Hebrides, they stand to pray; they sit to sing. Now, one side of the church threw their hands up in the air. They threw their heads back and you would almost declare that they were in an epileptic seizure. But they were not.

Oh, I can't explain it.

And on the other side, they slumped on top of each other. But God, the Holy Ghost moved. Those who had their hands in the air stayed that way for two hours. Now you try to remain like that with your hands up for a few minutes and you will find it very difficult. But you would have had to break their hands before you could have taken them down. Now, I can't explain it, yet this is what happened.

But the most remarkable thing that night took place in a village seven miles away from the church. There was not a single person from that village in the church. Not one person. Seven miles is how far this village was from us. While Donald McInnes was praying, the power of God swept through Scalpay, that is the name of the village. The power of God swept through the village, and I know for a fact, there was not a single house in the village that did not have at least one soul saved. Not a single house in the village.

A schoolmaster that night, looking over his papers fifteen miles away from this island—on the mainland. Suddenly, he was gripped by the fear of God.

And he said to his wife, "Wife, I don't know what's drawing me to Barvas, but I must go."

His wife said, "But it's nearly 10 o'clock and you're thinking of going to Barvas. I know what is on your mind. I know you are going out to drink. You are not leaving this house tonight!"

That was what she said to him, because he was a hard drinker.

Then he said to his wife, "I may be mistaken, oh, I may be mistaken, but if I know anything at all about my own heart and mind; I say to you right now that drink will never touch my lips again."

She said to him, "Well, John, if that's your mind, then go to Barvas."

So he got someone to take him to the ferry and to ferry him across to the island where I was. There I was conducting a meeting in a farmhouse at midnight and this schoolmaster arrives at the door. They made room for him and in a matter of minutes; he was praising God for salvation.

Now that's a miracle. I mean, you cannot explain it in any other way.

A father, a mother, two daughters, and a son were saved that night in this village. But another daughter was in the medical profession was in London. She was in London. A brilliant girl. She is walking down

Oxford Street after leaving a patient. Suddenly, the power of God arrests her.

She got home and went into a closet and cried to God for mercy and God saved her there in the closet. So, the whole family got saved!

My dear people, these are facts. I tell you these stories to honor God.

Today, that girl from London is the wife of a Baptist minister in Tasmania. He was in the Hebrides for two weeks at that time. Later, he asked for her hand in marriage. They married, and both of them serve the Lord in Tasmania today.

These are some of the remarkable movings of God.

That very night, a captain sailing a Clan Line cargo ship was saved, while sailing down to Mingulay at that very hour. The Spirit of God laid hold of him in his cabin.

The Spirit of God moved upon lobster fishermen in the sound. They had to leave their boats and their creels and make for the island. By morning, they were saved.

Oh, wouldn't it be wonderful if we saw God move in that way in this community? God could do it!

Author's Note Five:

Let's reset our focus here for a moment. What is the purpose of *The Revival You Want. The Revival You Need*!

How about this? Improvement through inspiration. Equipping through impartation.

While attaining everything the Hebrides Revival achieved would be outstanding. What they did to realize their mighty revival is a monumental undertaking. Doable, but not the level most are at. But all, by the grace and mercy of God, can improve. And massive leaps are achievable.

Here is what would help:

1. We need a Donald.

What an inspiring story. Donald, from the Hebrides Revival, was like gasoline on already ravenous flames. A flamethrower.

Find a Donald and come alongside that person as an encourager, prayer partner, maybe funding some of their needs/endeavors.

Or option two: become a Donald. Set yourself on fire, so people can watch you burn.

>
> Malachi 3:2
> "But who can endure the day of His coming? And who can stand when He appears? For He is like a refiner's fire And like launderers' soap."

Chapter 6.

Opposition Arises. Opposition Falls

I think one of the most outstanding things that happened, which happened in the parish of Arnot, will go down in history for as long as the Hebrides Revival is mentioned.

Now, I regret to say that here a certain section of the Christian church bitterly opposed me. Opposed by ministers who were born-again without question. They were God-fearing men, but for some reason or other, they came to believe that I was not sound in my doctrine because I preached the baptism of the Holy Ghost.

I proclaimed a Savior who could deliver from sin—glorious emancipation! And they got it into their minds that I was teaching absolute perfection or sinless perfection. A doctrine which I never taught, nor could I ever believe in.

Of course, I believe in conditional perfection: "But if we walk in the light as He is in the light, we have fellowship with one another, and the blood of Jesus Christ, His Son, cleanses us from all sin."

That is scriptural perfection! That is based on obedience.

But the dear men somehow believed, of course, not one of them ever listened to me. They listened to stories brought to them. So, they decided to make a special effort to oppose me.

To oppose me and they brought several ministers from the mainland, to this particular parish, to conduct meetings opposing Duncan Campbell and his revival.

Well, they came, and they were so successful in their opposition that very few people from this community came near any of my meetings. It is true that the church was crowded, and it is true that people were standing outside that could not get in. But these were people who came from neighboring parishes. Brought by coaches, brought by cars, and what have you. Yet there were very few from this village.

So one night, one of the elders came to me and said, "Mr. Campbell, there is only one thing that we can do. We must give ourselves to prayer. Prayer changes things."

Well, you know I am very willing to do that and said, "Where will we meet?"

"Oh," he said, "There is a farmer, and he is very willing to place his farmhouse at our disposal."

It was winter, and the church was cold. There was no heating in it. The people believe in a crowded church to provide its own heat.

But we wanted a warmer spot, and they approached the farmer. Now the farmer was not a Christian nor his wife, but they were God-fearing.

Now let me explain. You can be God-fearing and know nothing of salvation. There are thousands of people in upper Scotland who are God-fearing. They have family worship morning and evening. They would never dream of going out to work in the morning without reading a chapter of the Bible. And getting down on their knees to ask God to have mercy upon them and their family.

The man might have been drunk last night and may not come to the church, but he always reads the

Bible before going to work. That is why I believe that the average unsaved person in the Hebrides has a far greater knowledge of the Word of God than the average Christian anywhere else. I think I can say that, because of this custom of family worship.

This man had that going for him. Yet, he was not a Christian, but a God-fearing man. So we gathered at his house.

I would say there were about thirty of us, including five ministers from the church of Scotland. Men who had burdens, longings to see God move in revival. And we were praying and oh, the going was hard. At least I felt it to be hard.

Between 12 and 1 o'clock in the morning, I turned again to this blacksmith whom I have already referred to prior. Oh, he was a prince in the parish.

I said to him, "John, I feel that God would have me to call upon you to pray."

Up until then, he was silent. Then that dear man began. He must have prayed for about half an hour.

When he paused for a second or so and then, looking up towards the heavens and cried, "God, do

You know that Your honor is at stake? Do You know that Your honor is at stake? You promised to pour water on the thirsty and floods on the dry ground. God, You are not doing it."

Now, my dear people, could we pray like that? Ah, but here was a man who could. Here was a man who could.

He said, "There are five ministers in this meeting and I don't know where a one of them stands in Your presence, not even Mr. Campbell."

Oh, he was an honest man.

He continued, "But if I know anything at all about my own poor heart, I think I can say and I think that You know that I'm thirsty! I'm thirsty to see the devil defeated in this parish. I'm thirsty to see this community gripped as you gripped Barvas. I'm longing for revival and God, You are not doing it! I am thirsty and you promised to pour water on me."

He paused and then he cried, "God, I now take upon myself to challenge you to fulfill Your covenant engagement!"

Now it was nearing two o'clock in the morning.

What happened? The house shook. A jug on a sideboard fell onto the floor and broke.

A minister beside me said, "An earth tremor."

And I said, "Yes."

But I had my own thoughts. My mind went back to Acts Chapter 4 when they prayed, the place shook.

When John Smith stopped praying at twenty minutes past two, I pronounced the benediction and left the house.

What did I see? The entire community was alive. Men carrying chairs, women carrying stools.

And asking, "Is there room for us in the churches?"

And the Arnot revival broke out. And oh, what a sweeping revival! I do not believe there was a single house in the village that wasn't shaken by God.

I went into another farmhouse. I was thirsty. I was tired. I needed something to drink. So I asked for a drink of milk and I found nine women in the kitchen crying to God for mercy—nine of them!

The power of God swept and here was a little boy. Oh, he was kneeling by a pigsty and he is crying to God for mercy.

One elder goes over to him and prays over him and little Donald McInnes came to know the Savior. And I believe more souls were brought to Christ through that one lad's prayers than through the preaching of all the ministers from the island—me included. God used him.

He was the boy that prayed, "I gazed upon an open door."

Author's Note Six:

It is kind of a given that there will be opposition to any significant move of God. Even a small tent revival set up on a vacant lot in a city can be a magnet for naysayers. And then there are two other points I want to highlight from this chapter.

1. God fearing. Not saved.

It is interesting that Duncan Campbell pointed out that someone can be God-fearing yet not know Jesus as their Savior. Yet, we know in the book of

James that even the demons tremble—have the fear of God.

This subject could be forty pages. But I will not do that. So, Campbell pinpoints someone who reads the Bible every day, yet does not know Jesus.

One of the Godliest men I have ever known talked about one of the first churches he pastored. The way he tells it, it was like there was hardly anyone there that was born again. They attended church regularly and did all the church routine, but did not know Jesus.

He estimates that in the church in America, at a minimum, half of all churchgoers are not in right relationship with Jesus Christ.

This hell-bound half includes pastors, Sunday school teachers, worship leaders, and a lot of what we see as *good folks*.

Are you in right relationship with Jesus? Is the Holy Spirit living inside of you? Living in sin? On the prayer team?

The Bible says, "Examine yourselves to see whether you are in the faith. Test yourselves. Do you not know yourselves, that Jesus Christ is in you? — unless indeed you are disqualified."

Examine yourself!

And then, once we pass the examination, our focus shifts. From there, it is important to tune in to who is of the faith and who is not of the faith. It is a fine line to traverse. When trying to use discernment in this area, it is accurately achievable only through a deep, abiding relationship with the Holy Spirit.

Loving people enough to be concerned about their spiritual state, and then popping the hood to figure out what's really inside, is a challenge, no matter how close you are to God.

2. The Nobodies

This is my second go around on this subject. I could write fifty pages on this subject. Again, I will not do that.

It grips my heart how Campbell stepped back, with obvious Holy Spirit discernment, and then picks the right lay person.

Beautiful humility. So precious.

His step of humble obedience unleashes a level of Holy Spirit power few people will ever see in their entire life.

There has been a prophecy around for at least twenty years. I have heard it countless times. It is about the faceless, nameless prophets who will be the power-igniters behind the last great revival before Jesus returns.

Obviously, these people have names and faces and friends who know their names. Yet, as we look at people who are on the posters and those who have enough followers on Facebook to start a small country, we miss the blacksmith, two elderly ladies, and Donald McInnes.

Or we miss the guy who lives in his car and that eccentric dude who always seems to be on a different wavelength.

Maybe you are one of the faceless-nameless. Keep praying! God is looking at you.

3. Opposition

I attended the Brownsville Revival in 1998. Brownsville had a lifelong impact on my Christian life. I even became intrigued with the revival a few months before I got saved. So, it was a *witness* which helped draw me to the Lord.

There was a guy who had a prominent radio program at the time, and it seemed like his full-time job was to criticize what was going on at Brownsville. Was the revival perfect? Of course not. Was it a true move of God? Hands down, flat-out, yes!

I was at a small tent revival around twenty years ago. Some Mormons ended up in the bleachers, on the back row, and started talking to a lady.

The preacher stopped preaching, called them out, told them to stop, and said, "Get your own tent!"

So radio guy. Get your own tent. Go start your own revival. So, if you think something is not a true move of God, go start a real one.

Get your own tent.

So, we can expect opposition. Campbell did not attack those opposing him. He graciously said that they were believers.

He simply got himself a blacksmith who could pray a prayer which could cause the earth to tremor.

Another high bar. Prayer is going to be the key. And maybe God will send a faceless-nameless to your prayer gathering.

From Revelation 4

"After these things I looked, and behold, a door standing open in heaven... the twenty-four elders fall down before Him who sits on the throne and worship Him who lives forever and ever, and cast their crowns before the throne, saying: 'You are worthy, O Lord, To receive glory and honor and power; for You created all things, And by Your will they exist and were created.'"

Chapter 7.

Changing a Community

Now that night, the drinking house was closed. Yes, the drinking house was closed. Now sixteen years ago, in 1952, and it has never reopened since.

I was back some time ago and an old man pointed at the former drinking house, with its windows boarded up, and he said, "Mr. Campbell, do you see that house over there? That was the drinking house of the past. Do you know that last week at our prayer meeting, fourteen of the men who drank there are now praying men?"

Now people, that's revival. That is God at work. Miracles, supernatural, beyond human explanation—it's God.

And I am fully persuaded, dear people, that unless we see something like this happening, the average man will stagger back from our efforts, our conferences, conventions, and crusades; they will stagger back, disappointed, disillusioned, and despairing. But oh, if something happens that demonstrates God!

And the communists will hide in shame! I remember one night I saw seven communists and up until then they would spit in your face. Talk about religion being the dope of the masses. Educated men who would not go near a church.

But dear old Peggy had a vision one night and in the vision, she saw seven men from this community, from this center of communist activity, born again and becoming pillars of her father's church.

She sent for me and told me that God had revealed to her that He was going to move in this village. Oh, yes, there were communists there, godless men there. But what was that to God? When God begins to work, He would deal with them.

So, she kept on talking like that.

I said, "Peggy, I have no leadings to go to that village. You know that there is no church there, and the schoolmaster is one of those men who would never dream of giving me the schoolhouse for the meetings. I have no leadings to go."

And do you know what she said to me?

She said, "Mr. Campbell, if you were living as near to God as you ought to be, He would reveal His secrets to you, as well."

And I took her words as from the Lord. Oh, dear people, it is good to get a Word within you. It is good to see yourself as others see you. That was how I felt.

I said, "Peggy, would you mind if I call for the parish minister and together we will spend the morning with you in prayer?"

She replied, "Oh, I'll be happy too."

So, we came, and we knelt with her and she began to pray, and in her prayer, she said, "Lord, do You remember what you told me this morning when we had that conversation together?"

Oh, how near she was to God!

She also said, "I was telling Mr. Campbell about it, but he's not prepared to take it in. God, give him wisdom, because the man badly needs it!"

That was what she said! "The man badly needs it!"

And of course, she was speaking the truth. Of course, I needed it. I needed to be taught. But I was at the feet of a woman who knew God intimately. And I was prepared to listen.

So I said, "Peggy, when should I go to that village?"

"Tomorrow."

"What time?"

"Seven o'clock."

"Where am I to hold a meeting?"

Peggy said, "You go to the village and leave the gathering of the people to God and He will do it."

So I went to the village the next day and when I arrived, I found a crowd around a seven-room bungalow. I found five ministers waiting for me. And the house was so crowded that we could not get in. Indeed, we could not get near it. And I stood on a hill in front of the main door.

I gave out my text, "Truly, these times of ignorance God overlooked, but now commands all men everywhere to repent, because He has appointed a day on which He will judge the world in righteousness by the Man whom He has ordained."

I preached for about ten minutes, when one of the ministers came to me and said, "Mr. Campbell, do you remember what you spoke about at five o'clock this morning, out in a field, in that wonderful meeting, when you tried to help those that were seeking God?"

I happened to speak from John 10:27 "My sheep hear my voice; I know them and they follow me. I give unto them eternal life and they shall never perish. Neither shall any man pluck them out of my hand."

He said, "Could you go to the end of the house? Because there are some men there and we are afraid that they will go crazy because they are in such a state. Oh, they are mighty sinners and they know it. They are spoken of here as communists."

I went, and I saw seven men. The seven men that Peggy saw. And they were crying to God for mercy. The seven of them were saved within a matter of days. And if you go to that parish today, you would see a church, with a stone wall built around it, heated by electricity; all built by the seven men who became pillars in Peggy's father's church.

Oh, my dear people, that is God at work!

The minister saw two young men on their knees in the field crying to God and he recognized them as two pipers who were going to play at a concert and dance under the auspices of a nursing association off the island in his parish.

He turned to his wife and said, "Isn't that wonderful? There are the two pipers who were advertised to play in the parish hall tonight. Now there they are, crying to God for mercy. Come on, we'll go home. Then we will go to the dance and tell them what has happened."

So off he went. Oh, this was a man of God. Off he went with his wife. It was about fifteen miles.

He and his wife made it to the dance, and the people were not at all pleased with his appearing. He was there to disturb them. They knew he was not there to dance, for they knew the man.

However, he went in and when a lull came in the dancing, he stepped onto the floor and he said,

"Kinfolk, something very wonderful has happened tonight! The Smith pipers were to have been here tonight, the two brothers were to be here; they are crying to God for mercy in Barvas!"

Suddenly, stillness. Not a word.

And then he spoke again, "Young folks, will you sing a psalm with me?"

"Yes," said one young man, "If you lead the singing yourself."

And he gave out Psalm 50: "For God is depicted as a flame of fire."

And while singing that Psalm, the power of God fell upon the dance. And I understand that only three who were there that night remained unsaved.

The first young man to cry to God for mercy was really a boy and just last year, they inducted him into one of the largest parishes in Scotland.
He found the Savior that night with many others.
Oh, dear people, this is the doing of God.

You ask me, "What is the fruit of this type of movement?"

Not long ago, I asked the parish minister to give a report for the records of the church of Scotland. I asked him to give a report on the fruit of the revival. Did they stand? Any backsliding?

Now this is what he wrote: "I will confine my remarks to my own parish. I will allow the other ministers to give their own reports. But let me speak of my own parish. In a certain village, one hundred and twenty-two young people found the faith and I'm not talking about middle age or the old. They were wonderful, but I am reporting about the young people. One hundred and twenty-two young people, all of them over the age of seventeen. They found the Savior during the first day of the revival. Today, I can say that they are growing like flowers in the garden of God. There is not a single backslider among them."

Now, dear people, that is true, that is true.

Oh, if you knew the young people that have gone on from that to Bible colleges, who are today missionaries all over the world, who came into saving relationships during the revival. Growing, as he said, like flowers in the garden of God.

Oh, how we thank God for the stream of young people who have gone into the ministry.

I have sometimes talked about one young girl from Lewis. She was a young girl, a wild, wild girl, just seventeen years of age, and an outstanding singer. Frequently singing at big concerts in Glasgow. She was outstanding.

God saved her, and her life changed. She went to a Bible school and today I have no hesitation in saying that she is among the leading Bible expositors in Scottland. And that is saying a lot. She is presently in South Africa, addressing conferences and conventions. She has been instrumental in bringing blessings to scores of ministers and she was the fruit of the Hebrides Revival.

I will never forget the night that she prayed to get saved. She was brought up in a God-fearing home; her father and mother were not Christians, but they were saved at that same time.

And she was on her knees in her room at 3 o'clock in the morning and she prayed and she says, "God I'm turning from the ways of the world. You will never see me on a concert platform again. I will follow your people; I will be with them in the prayer meetings. I will never go back to the ways of the world. God, that is what I am purposing to do. Though at the end, You could have sent me to hell. That is what I deserve."

Oh, I remember the night that the Holy Ghost fell upon her at a communion service.

She lifted her two hands toward Heaven and she cried, "Oh, Bridegroom, Bridegroom of my heart, possess it all. Oh, Bridegroom, Bridegroom of my heart, possess it all!"

And the Holy Ghost came upon her in such a way that she began to cry, "Oh, God, You hold my hand! My young body cannot contain it! God! Hold me with Your hand! My young body cannot contain it!"

That was God. That is the fruit.

And what we are seeing today is God moving again among the teenagers.

And I asked a minister recently, "How can you explain it? Can you explain this movement in any way?"

He said, "Yes, I can. I can. I believe this has broken out because of the steadfastness of the young people who found the Savior during the big revival years ago."

The steadfastness of the young people. I can say without fear of contradiction that I can count on my ten fingers all who dropped off from the prayer meetings. Of course, they are scattered all over the world. They are in the mission fields and different places today, but according to the ministers in Lewis and other places; they are standing true to the God of the covenant and true to the Lord Jesus Christ.

Author's Note Seven:

I have been interested in revivals even before I was saved, as I had previously shared. One thing I have often thought, regarding revivals, is that the area near the revival should be affected; improved through the lens of scriptures. So, what would that look like?

1. Improved community.

When I attend the Brownsville Revival, my pastor and his wife went along with us.

My pastor was top tier in so many ways. I remember, but I do not know the details, he did some investigating in the neighborhood next to the church. He wanted to know if the people there were impacted by the revival.

If it was a Hebrides-style, wouldn't they pretty much all be saved and in ministry?

I do not remember what he concluded.

I know of a church, a wonderful church, that reports on Facebook and from the pulpit that they have been in revival for a year or maybe two. Now I would say God is unquestionably doing substantial things at the church and with the people who visit. But is the community improved in a Godly way?

Maybe minimally, but more likely, probably not. Still, that does not mean it is not a revival.

Yet, we should ask, "Why not?"

A week before starting the writing of this book, I was at a revival in Louisville, Kentucky. I mentioned it in the *Introduction* to *The Revival You Want. The Revival You Need!*

It was very small and took place on a corner lot on the westside of Louisville. This is the rough side of town. There was no real budget and there was a small awning tent, but basically, we sat in the grass on chairs—if you had brought your own. It was very casual and laid-back and the service sort of flowed with the Holy Spirit. Nothing like I had experienced before, yet I had a very rich and extremely enjoyable experience.

One night, the church minister shared a praise report about the absence of gunshots from the nearby party store for an entire week. He was not joking. He was serious.

One day, I walked the streets with some flyers I had printed. I knocked on doors, talking to people, and passed out the flyers. Of course, I prayed the whole time. And the pastor had challenged us to do some fasting during the revival.

A bunch of neighbors came to the revival, and an entire spectrum of things happened in their lives. I wasn't present on the last night when it reached its climax, but that neighborhood was undeniably influenced for the kingdom of God.

Was it Hebrides-style? No, but next year (unless Jesus returns), I will guarantee you, the bar will be raised!

Just as a side-note, a bonus: walking the streets, passing out flyers, in an era of Facebook friends, made a lot more impact than I had projected. The connecting with people aspect touched people's hearts. It certainly did mine.

This gets back to a theme of the book:

One more person.

One more inch.

Not only did the Hebrides Revival change the community in the throes of what God was doing. But the influence had staying power.

This is huge. In some ways more impressive than the revival itself. Especially considering the global impact that rippled out from these small islands.

Duncan Campbell, in his statistics gathering, does not offer any insight into the why or how.

As I pondered this, while certainly multi-faceted, my estimation would lean toward that it was the shepherds.

The people of God who were in leadership positions: the ministers, elders, deacons, and certainly lay people who loved God and loved people.

Campbell talked about many people in this category, during the revival, and acknowledge their faithfulness and work ethic. And Campbell exemplified the humble servant leader to those shepherds.

And then I have no doubt that the two sisters were prayer warriors to the end, the blacksmith stayed the course as a prince of a man, Peggy continued to hear from the Lord, and Donald's fire burned hot for the Lord all his days.

Psalm 63:1
"O God, You are my God. Early will I seek You. My soul thirsts for You; my flesh longs for You In a dry and thirsty land where there is no water."

Chapter 8.
A True Story. A True Revival

Now, my dear people, that is the story. And I tell it because I fear that another man has been going around the states, telling stories about the Hebrides Revival and writing books about it.

I regret to say that he made statements and wrote them in his books, which are not true or factual.

But this is the story of the revival that can bear the light of examination.

God did it. And we bless Him for it.

> From Isaiah 6
> "I saw the Lord sitting on a throne, high and lifted up, and the train of His robe filled the temple...I heard the voice of the Lord, saying: 'Whom shall I send, And who will go for Us?' Then I said, "Here am I! Send me.'"

Epilogue

A Beginning, Not an End

I would have no idea what other authors do regarding sitting down and reading their own work. For me, a typical pattern is that I do not read my book cover to cover until maybe two or three years after publishing.

The first reading is a surreal experience for me. Only an author who endeavors to tap into the Holy Spirit's guidance in the writing process can fully understand.

It is a weird experience to be reading your own work, while feeling a certain disconnection from the writing process. I recall, especially with my book, *Jesus at Walmart…a reed shaking in the wind*, I would cry in some of the same parts I cried while writing the book.

For *The Revival You Want, The Revival You Need!* I will read it soon after publishing.

Why change the pattern?

I want revival. I need revival. I need to be stirred to implement the same things I am encouraging you to do.

I have zero doubt that there will be a noteworthy revival before Jesus returns. And that day is rushing towards us.

When I read *The Revival You Want. The Revival You Need!*, if I am not stirred to action, I have failed.

I have asked myself the question repeatedly, "Are there any key reasons that such a powerful revival could happen in such an unexpected place?"

Yes, I have written a lot of methodology that we should plug into our quest to fire up revival. So, my question is a searching, a hunting down of anything else we can seize as a tool.

Two observations:

1. If I understand Duncan Campbell correctly, according to him, almost all the families in the Hebrides read the Bible daily, even if they were not saved. And even if they went to the bar and got drunk at night; they would still read the Scriptures.

This is very significant. The Bible is not just a book. It is living and active, sharper than any two-edged sword…

At my church, a guest speaker from World Missionary Press stressed the significance of sharing Scriptures with non-believers.

World Missionary Press prints ten million Scripture booklets a month, that look like tracks, but they are one-hundred percent Bible verses.

He said of the Scriptures, "It gives the Holy Spirit something to work with."

Exactly!

Because people of the Hebrides were devoted to reading the Bible, this boosted the Holy Spirit's power to eliminate sinful cravings as they cried out for mercy.

2. I was recently at a church in Franklin, Tennessee, which I had attended the previous Sunday. I was standing in the expansive foyer hoping to see someone I had met the previous Sunday.

I was standing in an open space, so I would have a good visual vantage point. Suddenly, for no apparent reason, a lady walks right up to me and started talking.

She just started talking. Truly strange. But soon I discovered this was a exceptional servant of the Lord.

I do not even remember how we segued into the discussion of the Hebrides. Yet I soon discovered that she had been a missionary there. Decades after the revival.

Something my new friend mentioned repeatedly was the isolation of the islands. Which would cause radically reduced distractions. First, the reduction of distractions because of that era in history and then they would not have a whole segment of distractions which pester us today.

Their isolation allowed them to more easily unplug from the things of the world. And made it easier to pursue the things of God.

My clarion call throughout the book has been: one more person, one more inch.

Courtney Dauwalter is likely the most extraordinary runner on the planet. She is an ultra-marathoner (think, one hundred miles plus), who is known for decimating the field. Like in a two-hundred-and-forty-mile race, beating her nearest challenger by eight hours. That is the entire field—men and women!

Courtney said, "In general, I think everyone's bars are just a little bit too low and that we should raise the bar for ourselves. We should go after the thing that sounds a little bit crazy or sounds a little bit too difficult and just see, because, why not?"

Raise the bar.

Because, why not?

Why?

There is a song I have been enjoying lately:

Come Away

Come away, my child, into the presence of the King
Come away, my child, into the presence of your King

And this is what He asks you to bring

Nothing

Nothing

Nothing

Except a life yielded to Him

Oh, let him give you a song to sing

Oh, let him give you a new life to bring

Oh, let him give you a freedom cry that must ring

And this is what He asks you to bring

Nothing

Nothing

Nothing

Except a life yielded to Him

My answer to the *why* is, "I want to have a life yielded, in every way, to God."

Here is the altar call. "Do you want to live a life fully yielded to God?"

One more insight before my, "Adios."

Chelsea Nolan is a musician whom I have heaps of appreciation for. Her line from her song *Build a Fire* resonates with me:

"You can tell a lot about a man by the way he builds his fire."

The Revival You Want. The Revival You Need! has given you a lot of fuel to ignite revival fires. You could delete all of my words, and with the words of Duncan Campbell, you would still have a bountiful amount of combustibles.

Duncan Campbell's way of shepherding the revival exemplified a beautiful, heart-touching humility. Blended with Godly wisdom. And he enlisted many people or recognized them as the fire starters. The words of Campbell only offer a snippet of who these people were at their core.

And I know for sure, we would do well, in our pursuit of revival, our desire to ignite some Holy Spirit fire, to emulate their lives.

"You can tell a lot about a man by the way he builds his fire."

A sustaining and powerful revival is built from the inside out. God will build you inside first—if you yield to him.

That is how God builds a fire.

And somewhere along the way in the interior building process, maybe sooner than you thought; more likely later than you thought; God, in His still small voice, will say to you:

"Build a fire!"

Adios

Dear Reader,

You are the fuel that ignites my desire to write. No readers, no writers.

A huge thank you for making the effort to let our lives intertwine. It is always a pleasure to hear from readers: rickleland1@outlook.com. And you can always stop by rickleland.com.

I am presently making a serious effort to learn Spanish. So, the idea of using the word *adios* just popped into my head.

Later I thought, "I wonder what *adios* really mean, since *Dios* means God?"

This is what it means, and this is my benediction/proclamation over your life: "I commit you to God."

Adios,

Rick Leland

P.S. Reviews are always appreciated!

The Revival You Need. The Revival You Want!

More Books by Rick Leland

Living the God-Imprinted Life

Jesus at Walmart…a reed shaking in the wind

Jesus at Walmart…the cost

Jesus at Walmart…fire on the Earth

Casting Out Demons for Fun and Profit

Forthcoming:

Jesus Doesn't Have Facebook…what the crap is going on?

Made in United States
North Haven, CT
05 September 2024